A little book of transcendence

Jakob Brønnum

Contents

1 – THERE AND HERE 5

Clouds and trees 6
Forgotten thoughts 7
Birds and aero planes 8
September 10
Cows looking into the late afternoon sun 12
The Bridge 15
The Old Boat in the Forest 16

2 – HERE 17

The Octogenarian 18
The Pregnant Woman 20
My Father 21
The poem about the embarrassment 22
Timelessness and purpose 23
Starry Night (van Gogh) 25
The painting on the sky, morning 26
Catch a thought 28
Losing count 29

3 – HERE AND THERE 31

Snow in August 32
Faces in the foliage 33
Winter dreaming 35
The Starlings on Good Friday 37
On taking place 38

4 – THERE 39

Reading Poetry 40
An Unfinished Poem 41
Telling Stories 42
Abandoned thoughts 43
On finding a dried leaf in an old dictionary 44
Caspar David Friedrich (Triptych) 46
The poem about Anubis 48
Notes and acknowledgements 49

1 – THERE AND HERE

Clouds and trees

The clouds look like they are trying
to pull the trees away with them

but they will not succeed

no matter how many clouds come this way
the trees will stay here.
They are mine

the trees are my mirrors
when I look at them and when I don't

The trees change much slower than time
and in a way no one notice right away

The clouds are mirrors too
but they change all the time

Forgotten thoughts

On a clothesline between the houses

it seems like somebody's thoughts
are hanging out to dry

the thoughts flutter in the wind
no one has time to take them in today

if anyone finally came for them
they would probably have atomized

fragmentized
be all unrecognizable

Birds and aero planes

All the birds and the aero planes
are flying in that direction

I wonder what's going on
There seems to be hole in the sky

It must be out there somewhere

I shall have to stand and watch
to see if they really disappear in there

I shall have to stand and watch
for as long as it takes in this vacuum space

2 The Beyond

Wonder what is beyond there

maybe it is a completely
different kind of light

guess it could also be a completely
different kind of time

By the way, I haven't seen any birds and
aero planes lately, come to think of it

wonder if they are all gone now

September

September is so transparently blue
I can hardly discern it

after a while
it reveals itself:

It looks backwards and forward
it bends over, just slightly
one cannot tell in which direction
sometimes it looks as if it is about to
fall over

then it rises
while it disappears

for the last time
tossing a blunt gesture of retreat

2 Blue phenomena

There are blue phenomena
one assumes one sees

like shadows floating in the snow
or the sky above

and daylight leaking out
in the late afternoon

but those are illusions
blue September is no illusion

it is so utterly blue
that you'd catch yourself

stretching out to touch
its illusionary body

Cows looking into the late afternoon sun

I pass the cows in the meadow
all of them facing the sun

I did not know they did that
or what's in it for them

they have been tolerantly cutting grass
for hours on end with their brutish
machinal teeth
now they are chewingly
processing the remains of the day,

all of them facing the sun as if it was calling them

2 *The Liturgy*

Cows are not philosophers
they have no idea of why Aristotle's Metaphysics
had to be placed at the end
of his shelf

they are gazing into an idea of a world
that does not exist

except in this liturgy of the communion
between great nothing and the eternal now

a realm of serenity I couldn't fathom
a field of light and timelessness, we would not grasp

even if we knew
how to reach for it aimlessly
like they do

2 The Passing

In a while, in the dark, it will still be there
the serenity, the idea
of the world that does not exist

the way it isn't here now. I wont

I, both existent and illusionary, shall have passed
maybe not unnoticed, but by all means

forgotten

The Bridge

The bridge between the two coasts
has been sitting there since I was a kid
longing to know

how they lived on the other side
or to just go up there
and stand above the world

only now I understand
that the bridge is no *still life*

as perceived from here, from there

in itself it is the symbol of moving so strong
that no one ever considers immobility
when admiring its elegant imagination

carrying the pillars of motion

The Old Boat in the Forest

The boats' mandorla-like shape
is evoking slow gliding on breathing water

a timeless image of time
mounting itself on the mind

an organic application
slowly downloading in me

as I approach the old boat resting
on the forest floor

the archetype of all other boats
evoking in the seer the water of life

2

Who leaves a boat
in the forest?

or was it dragged here
or was there onetime water underneath
carrying it and then gently setting it down

that has now disappeared
leaving to boat to thirst

Can you loose a boat
just like that?

could someone have forgotten it, just like that
(the trees certainly have not)

2 – HERE

The Octogenarian

1

little by little the other guests came
& joy strolling around the garden

Ah! Late summer's golden garden
(if somewhat bleached, you know how it is)

finally, the old ones come
he gets out of the car, wide-eyed
& she gets out of the car

waving and waving,
proud as an octogenarian

2

& began to look back to consider
the present through what has been

& all that will never come back
the privilege of an octogenarian

& the air disappear up into the
September sky

3

Soon enough the day becomes
homeless & universal

everybody's life is finally
captured in a prism

as if everybody turned around
at the same time
& as if everybody are turned around
at the same time
& as if time
turned everybody around

& the reality one cannot maintain alone
& now maintains itself fleetingly

this day truly was a facsimile
of later memories

The Pregnant Woman

I wanted to write a poem about the pregnant woman
that came out of the car, I thought
she was about to tumble, for a second
having forgot how equilibrium shifts all the time

but she didn't and I wanted to write a poem about why,
about the other person who helped her regain
her bodily balance

not yet born

not having readjusted, as she will be doing from now on
and forever, and her body tells her the story

that will have impregnated itself on her soul in due time
to adhere to the first parting of the other

My Father

If I saw him, how would I embrace him

would I gently touch his arm
to feel the shape of him
through the knitted sweater

would I cross the street if I saw him there
just to hear his voice

I shall never again hear his voice, his laughter
except in dreams
twenty years gone now
I still want to call him sometimes
in the morning

something about the light in the room
and Haydn's String Quartets

2

He did use to walk along right here
carrying home groceries

I'd cross the street
if I passed by one day

and realized I was on the wrong
side of the road

The poem about the embarrassment

It is the most apparent thing I leave behind
the sense of embarrassment

that's what I remember about leaving the room
no matter who was there

but you never really leave embarrassment behind,
do you? You carry it with you

the embarrassment, out in the night and solitude
it tends to be a heavy gadget to haul along

though you do find ways of carrying it
even if never truly elegant

from your own point of view that is
you are the one who knows what's in it

Some people do handle theirs smoothly I've noticed
I can only dream of getting there one day

but still, I take it home somehow, I manage
to at least make it home to nourish it

Timelessness and purpose

My son was very interested in crabs
when he was seven or eight

he'd stand on the wharf heaving them into his red bucket
he'd work for hours and hours

I was reading off and on, like it always is with children around
watching him from the dune while daylight changed

timelessness
slowly running out on him

At the end of the day, he'd throw them all back in
I was wondering about the purpose, the purpose of it all

My son is not interested
in crabs anymore (as far as I know)

I'm looking at him sometimes when I meet him
now grown-up, a man like myself,

to see if I can recognize the days of the crabs
manifest in his hands, in what he does

like in ways he goes about in his house dealing with
mugs, pots, and pans

The time may soon come when he calls me
about an excursion to the beach

relating something he felt while watching his child
during the enterprise of heaving crabs

out of the shallow water into a small plastic
bucket (probably a different color now) in the sun

I finally realize what the purpose is
and that timelessness is on me this time around

Starry Night (van Gogh)

The roar is immense, the sound waves
setting in motion this cosmos, this noise in your ear
stinging like dark green trees
much taller than spires, but not as alive
not as blessed, not as missed, not as uncertain
not as desperate, not as screaming, not as far away

the sound waves and the waves of light
merging in the seer's mind to form
this image of true wonder, this illusion of genius
that you alone know to be despair

There is a moon calling, the only voice
to be heard in this mercurial void tonight. It is the moon.

She might be the only one to be able
to take you down from flying with the universe
to be yourself again, tonight

calling you by your name and knowing what we cannot know
whether you've forgotten it and set all this in motion
to maybe get back on track to
yourself or you remember it all too well
but just haven't heard it said, for a while

The painting on the sky, morning

What sombre voice from the sky this morning
it is just like a painting by Constable

like a long-lost thought reminiscent of doubtless mornings
of childhood, happily ingrained in oneself

the little boy coinciding with the world's act of becoming:
Both prisoner and free

2 The Moment

Is it a depiction of the moment
with the moment for once consistent with the idea of itself
and not something you know
only as it its gone?

are the sky and my response
reflective of a mood
I just cannot capture in words
so I try calling it a painting instead?

Is this the lead to a trait of my character
not fully recognized
an immaterial gateway sliding open?

What is it this vast cover of wordlessness
covered in recognizable surface colors
trying to tell me now I it is understood that I try to listen?

Catch a thought

Snowflakes come down from above
like thoughts out of nowhere

they even respect the silence
of the afterthought, before the fact.

Look someone is stretching out
to maybe catch one of them

(might be me)

I always forget how much hands
act like thoughts themselves

they too never manage to grab
a thought and make it sit still

to watch it as it slowly dissolves
into time and white noise

Losing count

the sudden greying of daylight
& then the rain
finally, lightning strikes

I was trying to count the seconds
but before I reach the thunder

I'm again emerged in the den of childhood impressions
blurring this genuine cosmic moment
in time and in me

& now I lost the count
& while trying to remember where I was

there it comes, the thunder roaring

3 – HERE AND THERE

Snow in August

Snow in August right outside my window
gently dancing towards the ground
in the illuminated morning
last winter rushing in
almost forgotten by now

how did we actually make it
through those tunnelly months?

the coming winter, too
points its finger at me

mocking these crystalline passages
punctuating the epiphany with freezing reality

Faces in the foliage

Sometimes I see faces in the foliage
right before me, emerging

particularly when I pass trees
that I know well. There are a few

They form themselves in the depth
of the green sprawl, like sketches, borrowing

here, a little dark shade
there, some green light

The faces have patient eyes
are their mouths silently screaming?

Some have wise foreheads
others have clearly led a life of pain

2

Sometimes faces form themselves
in the foliage
insisting yet meek

very rarely faces you know
most often just faces

carrying the idea

of faces, sharing the realm

with the foliage
in its turn carrying the idea of the tree
of life

3

Sometimes faces open a door
into the timeless

and to the need for patient voices
and to the knowledge of how to caress someone
with a gesture or a word

there has never been anything else but faces
as long as symbols of existence stretches
back into time, never anything else in its place

as long as there have been humans dreaming
in their sleep. There never was anybody
that did not look like this

Winter dreaming

With everything turning into water
and to music made by
water

me, I'm looking out into the pale morning
as if I had forgotten something

and I had, I had forgotten my face
in the wind

2

The world has become thoroughly yellow
a very pale, a frail yellow, a squeaky yellow

with absolutely no energy to spare
a celestial memory loss

just before it all begins to burn
turning orange, on the path to red

with everybody closing their eyes
as its complementary colour takes over

3

the seasons never remember
their brothers and sisters

they only prophecy
about their own second coming

but time always has a hand in it too

and it turns out to be altogether
something else. In a short while

the world will be made of foliage changing hue
and texture by the minute soaking up

the remaining water music
and all the colours around it as well

The Starlings on Good Friday

Flocks of starlings on Good Friday
dodging traffic on the highway.

Liberal democracy might not last forever
every year daylight returns

while the grass retains its wintery brown for yet a while.
There are voices I prefer not to live without

I seem to invoke them mindfully
as the wind
carries assorted soundbites back to me.

The starlings, already much better at maneuvering April
than I will ever be, awestruck as I remain
by the power of the wind

not owning the wind like a winged creature
I'm deemed to just follow traffic

On taking place

Every time I come to a place
and start unpacking
putting it in order with a satisfied mind
and a glance
in my imaginative mirror of vanity
seeking out a place for every little thing
for it to lie and look
as if it has found its position
in life

every time a feeling seep in I will not
at first acknowledge
but after a while I know this
is not going to last

I know my attempt to acquire this place
is doomed in advance
me and my stuff are homeless

I can't take place

4 – THERE

Reading Poetry

Some of the images seem to be placed
on or outside the thing itself
like a sticker

the question is if
it is one of those stickers
you can never quite get off the surface
like a price tag on a used paperback

it leaves a little white scrap left and a mark
of your nail

2

The worst thing is
you cannot know if the sticker comes off
until you try
and you must try

you have to know
if this is really the poem

or if there is a fuller, undisturbed picture
to be attained by scratching the surface ever so gently

An Unfinished Poem

I am homeless like an unfinished poem
trying to find a place to stay

to start searching for its form
that has hidden itself
that is sprawled out
or chipped into fragments

under words that are already there
and all the words

that as yet have not come

Telling Stories

I know now why I prefer to have used things around me
and not just brand new, like porcelain
with a small crack in one corner

a rift in the plastic coating somewhere upon a bowl
New things don't tell stories. They just sit there

not even waiting to be used, tense, unintelligent
while you stove them away, as if nothing ever happens

Then somehow one day, there it was, piece-fully
on the floor

all laughing and crying
or hiding

its chip by turning
the back on you in the cupboard

trying not to give away its plot twist, yet

Abandoned thoughts

Some of the thoughts are standing in the field
as if they have been forgotten
this happens to a lot of thoughts

we have them and we forget them, and they get

very lonely

because every thought contains promise

because even thoughts cannot go
completely away

On finding a dried leaf in an old dictionary

When it was put there
by me or someone else who owned the book before

it was nothing but a neat place
to preserve a colored leaf - a voluminous book

you don't use all the time
speechlessly surveying the past and present

from its abode on the bookshelf
until suddenly called for.

Now it is much more than that. The dry leaf
is a tender, a rustic voice

painstakingly retelling a story
about an autumn day long since past

as if it were
enacting an ideally parallel occurrence

to the demand for a word or a meaning you simply can't recall -
you slam the book shut

not having found the expression
you know it has to be in there somewhere

vainly wishing your command
of language one day

would be like picking up fallen leaves
from the ground at will

saving them in a place you'd just as soon forget
trusting they will show up exactly when you need them

Caspar David Friedrich (Triptych)

Sometimes it seems he did not find the motives
they found him, the sought him up
to make him speak in a low tone of voice
almost like an organ slowly grinding in the distance

the way the funeral procession is literally moving
in front of our eyes, despite the fact
that it is a painting

and the scenery set inside ancient ruins
no longer used for the purpose

of burial, still used for the purpose of
illuminating the decay of the body

he did not find the motives, they found him
and now the painting is waiting for me to find it
to be illuminated by what cannot radiate

2

They way the two people
are standing in the shimmering light
contemplating the moon

next to the crooked trees
that's when you learn to look into the soul of a stranger
as well as of a friend:

By the symbolic gestures of the organic mess
by what is known to have been
but now is stale

like when you know something is over
by the way it changes shape and form
never to change again

All the while the moon continues its learned pilgrimage
ensuring nobody ever forgets contemplating
the face of eternity

3

The way he stands above the clouds
staring out into the valley covered in greyish white
knowing that he is looking right into

his own soul catching a rare glimpse
of something there might not be words for
but he doesn't care about words

he is hunting the foundation of the bottomless

he wants to secretly braze the self
that keeps disappearing in a pit of the psyche

he cannot frame in any other way

The poem about Anubis

Anubis is the Greek name for an Egyptian god
the god of mummification, of death,
of the walkway across to the second floor

through all of the royal apartments, throughout
the slow movement of Mahler's 5th, god of vomiting
just before death, and of meltdown immediately after

god of cemeteries, and all history's foggy, gothic necropolis trees
god of those who do not visit their father in the graveyard
god of those who burn their relatives for convenience's sake

some would call him a dog head
but that could be to go too far (or not far enough)
Anubis is Anubis, the Egyptian god with the Greek name

covering the entire Mediterranean basin
with a stench, deeper than decay, fiercer than ammoniac
more profound than the smell of fever

Notes and acknowledgements

On finding a dried leaf in an old dictionary has been published in Beyond Words Literary Magazine, *Starry Night* in The Ehphrastic Review, *Timelessness and purpose* has been published in the anthology New Contexts 4 (Coverstory Books) and *The poem about Anubis* in Line-Breaks by Coverstory Books

Starry Nights alludes to the painting by van Gogh (1889).

The paintings of Caspar David Friedrich alluded to in the poem are: 1) Abbey in the Oak Forest, 1809–10, 2) Two Men Contemplating the Moon, ca. 1825–30, 3) Wanderer above the Sea of Fog, 1818

On taking place, Abandoned thoughts and The poem about Anubis first appeared in other versions in the Danish in my collection Virkeligheden 2.0 (Reality 2.0, 2019)